Text and design copyright © 2001 by BBC Worldwide Limited. All rights reserved. Published by Scholastic, Inc, by arrangement with BBC Worldwide Limited. SCHOLASTIC and associated logos are trademarks and/or registered trademarks of Scholastic, Inc. The Blue Planet © BBC 2001. Blue Planet word mark and logo are trademarks of the British Broadcasting Corporation.

Cover Design by Joyce White
12 11 10 9 8 7 6 5 4 3 2 1   2 3 4 5 6 7/0
Printed in Hong Kong
First Scholastic printing, February 2002
ISBN 0-439-33413-6

SHARK WATCH

CONTENTS

What are sharks?   2
Ocean killers   4
Shark attack!   6
Swimming and breathing   8
Shark senses   10
How sharks hunt   12
Eggs and young   14
The history of sharks   16
Sharks in danger   18
Shark tales   20
Save the shark   22
Mackerel sharks   24
Great white sharks   26
Megamouths and basking sharks   28
Carpet sharks   30
Whale sharks   32
Hornsharks   34
Angel sharks and saw sharks   36
Ground sharks   38
Requiem sharks   40
Hammerhead sharks   42
Dogfish, frilled sharks, and six-gilled sharks   44
Fact file   46
Glossary   47

Some words in this book are shown in **bold**. These words are defined in the glossary at the back of this book.

WHAT ARE SHARKS?

The word "shark" is enough to send shivers down most people's spines. The thought of being helpless and alone in the water and suddenly seeing a fin attached to a sleek body, cutting through the waves toward you, is terrifying. And those teeth! The great white's teeth are razor sharp and each can be as long as a man's finger. Its jaws are powerful enough to cut through bone. But of the 450 or more **species** of sharks, the vast majority are harmless to humans. These species are divided into eight groups:

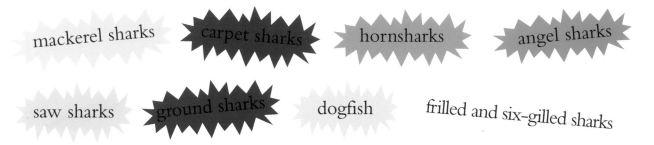

mackerel sharks   carpet sharks   hornsharks   angel sharks

saw sharks   ground sharks   dogfish   frilled and six-gilled sharks

Each group is described later in this book, starting on page 24.

Like all fish, sharks are **vertebrates**, which means that they have a skeleton and a backbone. But unlike most fish, the shark has a skeleton that is not made of bone. It is made of a gristly, flexible material called **cartilage**, the same substance that makes up the hard part of the human ear. Instead of smooth scales, the shark's skin is rough, because it is covered by tiny, tooth-like structures, each one like a backward-pointing thorn.

a Caribbean reef shark pursuing a school of fish

There are sharks in every ocean, but more live in warm waters than in chilly polar seas. Some, such as angel sharks, stay in shallow water, but there are sharks in deep water, too. The Portuguese shark has been found living at depths of more than 8,200 feet. Fast swimmers, such as mako sharks, swim across the open ocean, moving from one feeding ground to the next.

a gray reef shark patroling a coral reef

OCEAN KILLERS

The majority of sharks are fast-moving and sharp-toothed. They are perfectly designed for life as ocean killers. Their streamlined bodies allow them to speed through the water with little effort. Their huge jaws open wide to gulp down large **prey**. And their triangular teeth, with sharp, jagged edges, can slice through almost anything. Sharks have the largest brains of any fish, which enable them to outthink their victims.

the huge jaws of a great white shark

But not all sharks are speedy **predators**. Carpet sharks have flattened bodies edged with ragged flaps of skin. They spend much of their lives lying in wait for prey on the seabed.

a lesser spotted dogfish, one of the smaller sharks

The biggest fish in the sea is the mighty whale shark. It can measure up to 60 feet in length and weigh four times as much as an African elephant. But not all sharks are giants. Like many of its relatives, the lesser spotted dogfish is only a little over 3 feet long. And the spined pygmy shark measures only 10 inches — roughly the length of a man's foot.

SHARK ATTACK!

The most dangerous species of shark are the great white, the tiger shark, and the bull shark. These three are responsible for most of the attacks on humans.

Every year, there are between 70 and 100 shark attacks around the world. Some victims escape, but often they suffer terrible injuries. An Australian man named Rodney Fox was spearfishing when he was seized by a great white shark. He fought back, trying to punch the shark's eye — which is a good way to deter a shark from attacking — and managed to free himself. Fortunately he was rescued quickly, but his wounds needed 462 stitches.

shark attack victim Rodney Fox with a photograph of his injuries

In another attack, a young boy named Ray Short was swimming off a beach near Sydney, Australia, when a great white grabbed his leg. As he struggled, a wave washed him and the shark closer to shore, and rescuers began pulling him to safety. The boy was dragged onto the beach, but the shark came with him, its teeth still sunk into his leg. The boy needed 14 operations but he survived the attack. Others have not been so lucky.

Although being caught in the teeth of a great white is a terrible ordeal, it is also very unlikely to happen. Many more people are killed each year by poisonous snakes than by sharks. And people kill more than 100 million sharks annually, while sharks only kill between 5 and 15 people!

a pack of sharks tearing at bait

SWIMMING AND BREATHING

Like all fish, sharks breathe by taking oxygen from seawater. Water flows into the shark's mouth, over its **gills**, and out again through its **gill slits**. As water flows over the gills, oxygen is taken out, and carbon dioxide is released into the water.

Many sharks need to keep moving forward all the time so that water flows into their mouths and they can continue to breathe. But some bottom-dwelling sharks, such as the perfectly **camouflaged** wobbegong, can pump water over their gills using special muscles.

a wobbegong shark, which does not need to keep moving forward in order to breathe

A shark swims by moving its whole body from side to side and thrusting with its big tail. The shark's body is very flexible and can bend almost in half to change direction or snap at prey. A shark can use its fins as brakes, spreading them out to stop quickly.

Sharks don't sleep, but they can slow their bodies down and rest for a short time. Most resting sharks need to lie facing into a current of moving water to keep oxygen passing over their gills.

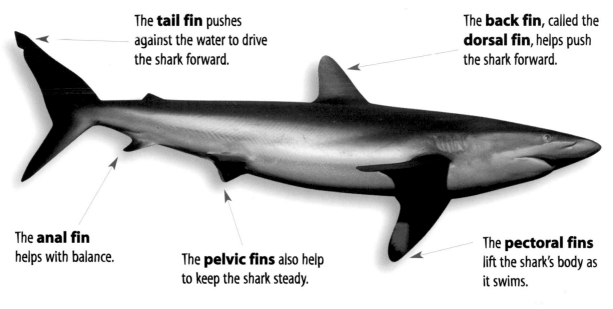

The **tail fin** pushes against the water to drive the shark forward.

The **back fin**, called the **dorsal fin**, helps push the shark forward.

The **anal fin** helps with balance.

The **pelvic fins** also help to keep the shark steady.

The **pectoral fins** lift the shark's body as it swims.

a resting gray reef shark

Sharks have excellent hearing. They are particularly attracted to irregular sounds, such as the splashing of an injured fish. For this reason, it is better to swim with smooth, rhythmic strokes when in the water with a shark!

Sharks also have highly sensitive noses. They can detect tiny amounts of substances, such as blood, in the water, and track them from over a mile away.

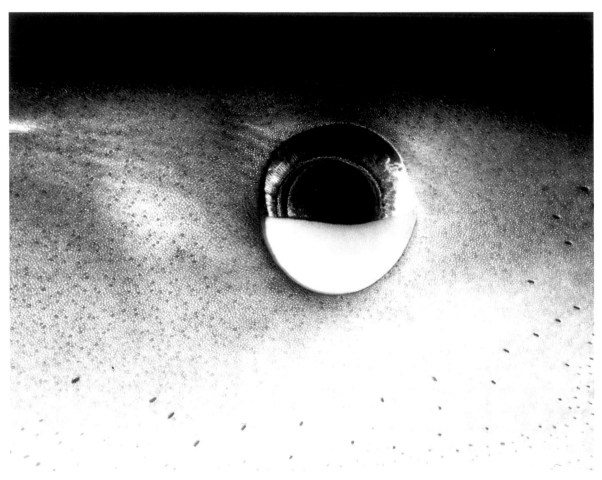

a nictitating membrane covering a tiger shark's eye

Once the shark is close to its prey, its keen eyesight is important. Most sharks have eyes on the sides of their heads. They can see forward and backward and up and down, but they can't judge distance well. The hammerhead is unique in having one eye at either side of an especially elongated head, which gives it a wider field of vision. Sharks do have eyelids, but they don't close completely, so some sharks have an extra eyelid, called a **nictitating membrane**. This comes across the eye to protect the shark when it is attacking a struggling victim.

a hammerhead shark

Sharks can also taste and touch, and they have two other special senses. One is the **lateral line system**. This is a row of sensitive nerve endings running along each side of the shark's body, from the head to the pelvic fin. The lateral line enables the shark to sense any movement in the water.

A shark's other special sense is its ability to detect the tiny electrical charges given off by other creatures. Sharks achieve this through unique sense organs in their snouts, called **Ampullae of Lorenzini**. Using these, the shark can find a fish buried in the seabed.

HOW SHARKS HUNT

All sharks are **carnivores**. While many sharks feed on shellfish, fish, and squid, others attack prey as large as whales, sea lions, and even other sharks. Fast swimmers, such as the mako, chase their victims until they are close enough to attack. To eat large prey, smaller sharks must disable it first by biting off a tail or a fin. Bottom-dwelling sharks lie in wait on the seabed. When an unsuspecting victim comes near, the shark opens its mouth wide to suck in its prey.

the small, sharp teeth of the swell shark, designed for holding slippery fish

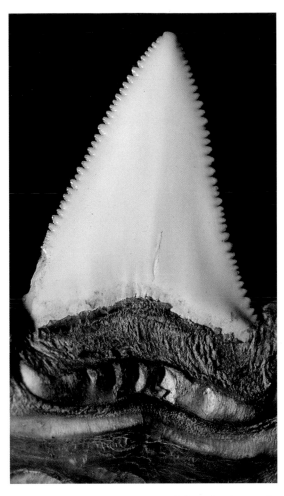

a great white shark tooth

Sharks' teeth vary in size and shape according to their diets. Large predators have big, triangular, knife-like teeth with jagged edges. The great white, for example, has teeth that can be 3 inches long, as long as a human finger. Shellfish eaters, such as the nurse shark, have broader, flatter teeth for crushing their hard-shelled meals. A tiger shark's teeth have sharp, backward-pointing tips that can hold slippery prey, and rounded bottoms for crushing **carrion**, hard shells, and anything else the tiger shark feels like biting.

Sharks' teeth are arranged in rows, one behind the other. If a tooth wears out or breaks, another moves into place from the row behind. A new tooth then grows in the back row to replace the one that has moved. A shark may use up to 20,000 teeth during its lifetime.

the perfectly adapted teeth of a tiger shark

13

EGGS AND YOUNG

There are three different ways that sharks produce young. Some, such as hornsharks, produce eggs in tough cases, which are left on the seabed. The egg contains a rich ball of food, called a yolk, which feeds the baby shark until it has grown enough to break out of the shell. Little tendrils at the corners of the egg case attach themselves to seaweed or other objects so the egg isn't carried off into deep ocean waters, where the young shark would not be able to survive.

the egg case of a larger
spotted dogfish

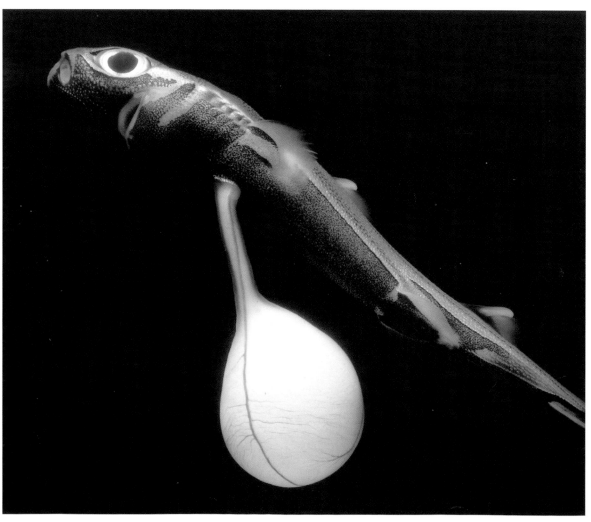

a baby lantern shark still attached to its yolk sac

Others, such as tiger and mako sharks, have a different system. They produce eggs that have just a thin skin around them instead of a tough case. These eggs stay inside the female's body while they develop. The young still feed on their egg yolk, but once they have finished their own food supply, they break out and gobble up other eggs. After the mother has given birth, her young are left to find food for themselves.

a baby swell shark developing in its egg case

Requiem and hammerhead sharks' eggs develop inside the female's body as well, but these young sharks have **placentas** instead of yolks. The placenta transfers food and oxygen directly from the mother to the baby shark. The mother then gives birth to live young, usually in safe, shallow water. Here, the tiny sharks can feed on shrimp and small fish until they are ready to swim into deeper water.

The first sharks lived about 400 million years ago — 150 million years before the first dinosaurs — and they have changed amazingly little since. One of the earliest was a shark called cladoselache. Like most sharks today, it had a torpedo-shaped body, two fins on its back, and a large tail. It fed on squid and fish.

An ancestor of the great white, named megalodon, died out about 12,000 years ago. Scientists think it may have been twice the size of today's great white.

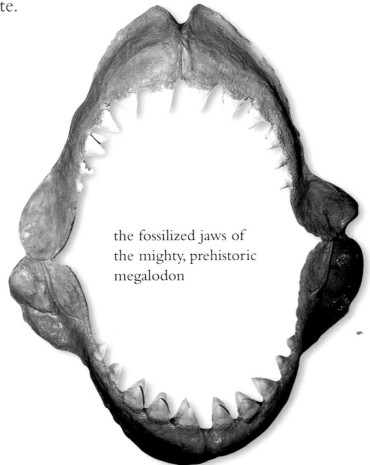

the fossilized jaws of the mighty, prehistoric megalodon

Today, the largest sharks are still at the top of their food chain. A shark may eat tuna, which in turn feed on squid, which feed on shrimp, which feed on algae, and so on. Every plant or animal is part of a food chain. Because sharks are at the top of their food chain, they can eat almost any other creature, but no other creature eats them. From tiny plankton to huge elephant seals, no prey seems too big or too small for sharks.

right: a caribbean reef shark, which has been caught on a line and attacked by a huge bull shark

shark fins drying in the sun

Sharks' worst enemies are humans. Every year, at least 100 million sharks are caught for sport, pleasure, or commercial purposes. Shark skin can be made into shoes, belts, or wallets. Shark liver oil is used in cosmetics, medicines, and other products, and shark flesh is eaten in many countries. Shark fin soup is a popular delicacy in Asia.

Sharks are usually trapped in nets or caught on baited long-lines — very long pieces of rope with baited hooks attached at evenly spaced distances. Smaller sharks are also caught in giant fishing nets that are dragged over the seabed.

right: a shark that has been caught on a baited long-line

SHARK TALES

Sharks have long been the subject of stories and legends. In New Guinea, it was once believed that sharks had magic powers and should never be harmed. In the Solomon Islands, the natives worshiped a shark god to whom they made human sacrifices. And, in Hawaii, people believed that there was a shark king who lived near their islands. They sent young men to prove their strength by fighting the king's subjects — live sharks — in wooden pens on the seabed.

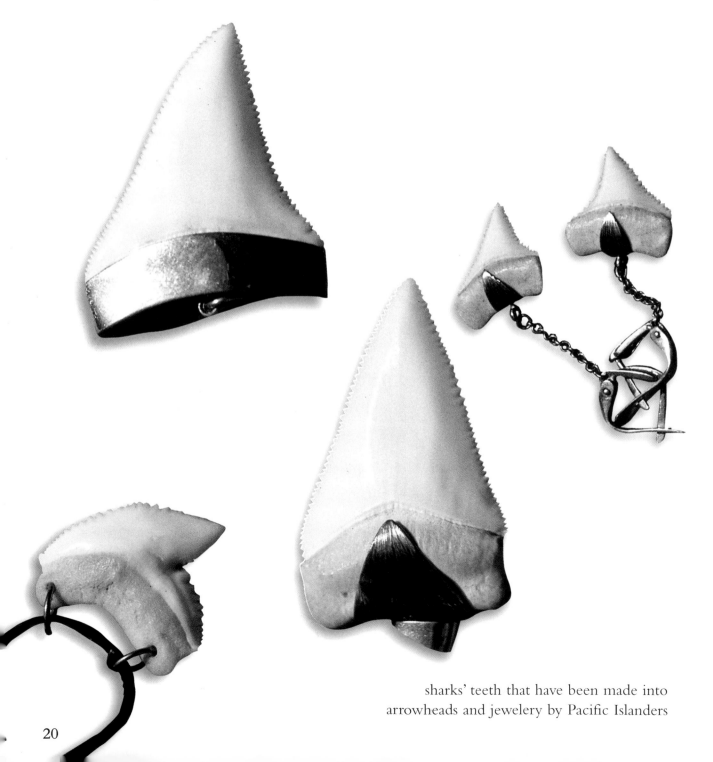

sharks' teeth that have been made into arrowheads and jewelery by Pacific Islanders

a great white investigating a cage containing a marine biologist

Today, man-eating sharks appear in films and books. There are many myths and horror stories about shark attacks off the coasts of California, Florida, and Australia. But, although big sharks are dangerous, most are very unlikely to attack unless disturbed.

As we find out more about sharks, we realize that they are not evil monsters, but creatures perfectly adapted to life as ocean predators.

SAVE THE SHARK

Because sharks have such a bad reputation, most people don't care if they are killed, trapped in nets, or overfished. But many species of shark are in danger of disappearing. Sharks do not produce large numbers of young each year, and commercial fisheries take far more sharks than can be replaced. Many more are caught by accident in nets put down to catch tuna or squid. Others are killed by pollution.

Sharks deserve to be treated with more care. They are an important part of the balance of life in the sea. They ensure that the populations of the animals on which they prey do not become too large, and they provide a valuable service by eating sick or dying creatures that might otherwise spread disease. If sharks are to survive, they need people to understand them rather than fear them.

Sharks are best observed with a knowledgeable guide.

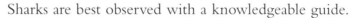

right: a tiger shark, one of the few species not currently endangered

MACKEREL SHARKS

Mackerel sharks have two dorsal fins, an anal fin, and a long mouth. There are 16 different kinds of mackerel sharks. The crocodile shark is the smallest at just over 3 feet long. Most mackerel sharks are much larger.

The shortfin mako's tapered body is designed for speed.

One mackerel shark, the shortfin mako, is the fastest of all sharks. It has been observed traveling at speeds of up to 55 miles per hour — that's as fast as a cheetah can run on land. It can hunt other fast swimmers such as tuna, swordfish, and mackerel.

One of the reasons for the mako's speed is its special blood circulation system. Most sharks are **cold-blooded**, but the mako is "partially warm-blooded" because its circulatory system keeps its body temperature higher than that of the surrounding water. Since the mako's muscles are warm, it can move more quickly than most cold-blooded sharks.

Another mackerel shark, the sand tiger, is a bulkier fish. It is slow-moving and spends much of its day resting in the shelter of a cave or rock crevice. At night it gulps air from the water surface and is able to stay completely still without sinking. It holds the air in its stomach to keep itself afloat. The sand tiger catches herring, bluefish, butterfish, snapper, hake, eel, squid, and shellfish with its long, sharp teeth, before swallowing them whole.

right: a sand tiger shark

Great white sharks

The great white shark of the mackerel group is the largest predatory fish. It can measure up to 30 feet in length and can weigh as much as 3.2 tons — more than 40 average humans. It is the only shark that regularly hunts marine **mammals** such as seals, sea lions, otters, and even small whales. Great whites are also one of the sharks most often involved in attacks on humans. Some experts think that great whites don't mean to hunt humans, but mistake them for seals or sea lions. A great white is the only shark ever seen **spy hopping** — peering out above the surface of the water to locate prey, such as seals, basking on rocks.

Thanks to its 3,000 teeth and mighty jaws, a great white can eat huge meals very quickly. Its bite is at least 15 times more powerful than a human's. When a great white attacks, its jaws extend forward. The lower jaw holds the prey while the upper jaw and teeth do the cutting.

a great white shark

a great white rearing above the waves

Great whites aren't really white at all — they are gray. Their undersides are pale, which helps the sharks hide from their victims, because the pale color is hard to see against the light surface of the water. Its torpedo-shaped body, crescent tail, and pointed snout enable the great white to cut through the water with terrifying speed.

Megamouths and basking sharks

a megamouth shark

The mackerel shark group also includes two sharks as large as, although less terrifying than, the great white — the basking shark and the megamouth. The megamouth was only discovered in 1976. These sharks can reach more than 16 feet in length but are also timid, which is probably why only about 14 of them have ever been spotted. True to its name, the megamouth does have an enormous mouth. Over 3 feet wide when open, it contains as many as 100 rows of teeth. The megamouth lives in deep water but sneaks up near the surface at night, following the tiny shrimplike **krill**, a type of **plankton**, that it eats in huge quantities.

The basking shark is the second largest fish in the sea, after the whale shark. It can reach 50 feet in length — that's longer than a bus. Like the megamouth, it feeds on plankton, which it filters from the water with the **gill rakers** in its mouth. Gill rakers are tiny, toothlike structures inside the shark's gills, which act like a giant sieve.

a basking shark filtering microscopic food from the water

CARPET SHARKS

Carpet sharks are bottom-dwellers with flattened bodies. There are 33 different kinds of carpet sharks.

The carpet shark group includes a range of different-sized creatures, from the collared carpet shark, which is only 35 inches long, up to the gigantic whale shark. Most carpet sharks live in tropical and **temperate** waters.

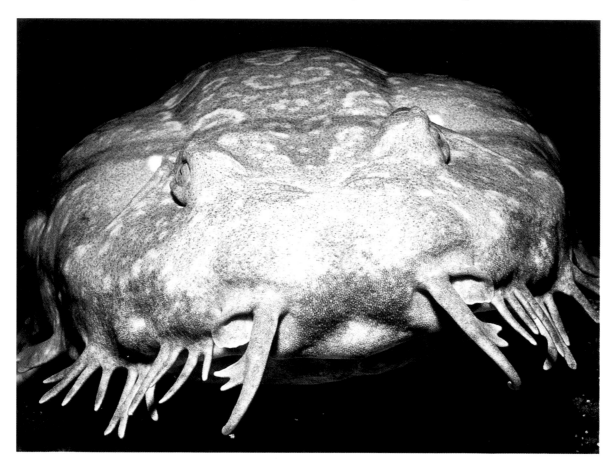

a wobbegong shark

One carpet shark, the wobbegong, really does look like a carpet. The ragged, frilly edges of its body give it the appearance of a frayed rug when it lies half-hidden in the sand. The flaps of skin around its mouth attract prey, such as crabs and lobsters, which then get snapped up if they come too close.

a nurse shark

Some of the most common carpet sharks are nurse sharks, which live in coastal waters and around coral reefs in the Atlantic Ocean and Caribbean Sea. During the day they hide in caves, but at night they are fierce hunters, preying on fish and shellfish. Fleshy flaps near the nurse shark's nostrils help it sniff out prey. The name "nurse shark" comes from their tendency to suck bait on fishing lines, like babies sucking on their bottles.

Some carpet sharks, like the epaulette shark, are able to "walk" across the seabed, using their strong pectoral fins like legs.

an epaulette shark

Whale sharks

The whale shark is not only the largest carpet shark but the largest of all living fish. Whale sharks can reach 60 feet in length — that's longer than a truck. The whale shark's huge jaws are filled with as many as 300 rows of tiny teeth, each one only about 1/8 inch long. It filters plankton from the water, but also sucks in larger food such as sardines. Water flows in through the whale shark's mouth and out through its gill slits, where any food items get caught in the sievelike mesh between the gills before being swallowed.

The whale shark is quite rare. Only about 100 have been sighted since it was first discovered in 1828.

HORNSHARKS

Hornsharks have a spine on each of their back fins.
There are only eight species of hornsharks.

Hornsharks' spines, from which they get their name, can be stuck up straight to scare off attackers. Hornsharks are also known as bullhead sharks because of their large, square-shaped heads — very different from the pointed snout of the typical shark.

Like all hornsharks, the Port Jackson shark spends much of its life on the seabed. It does not need to keep swimming to breathe because it has special muscles that pump water through its gills. It has sharp spines in front of its dorsal fins that stick out when the shark is threatened. The Port Jackson shark feeds at night, gobbling shellfish, such as sea urchins, crabs, and prawns, which it crushes with its large, flattened teeth. Port Jackson sharks reach a length of over 5 feet.

a Port Jackson shark

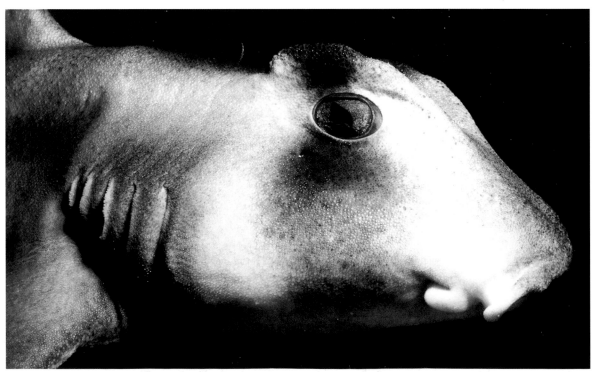

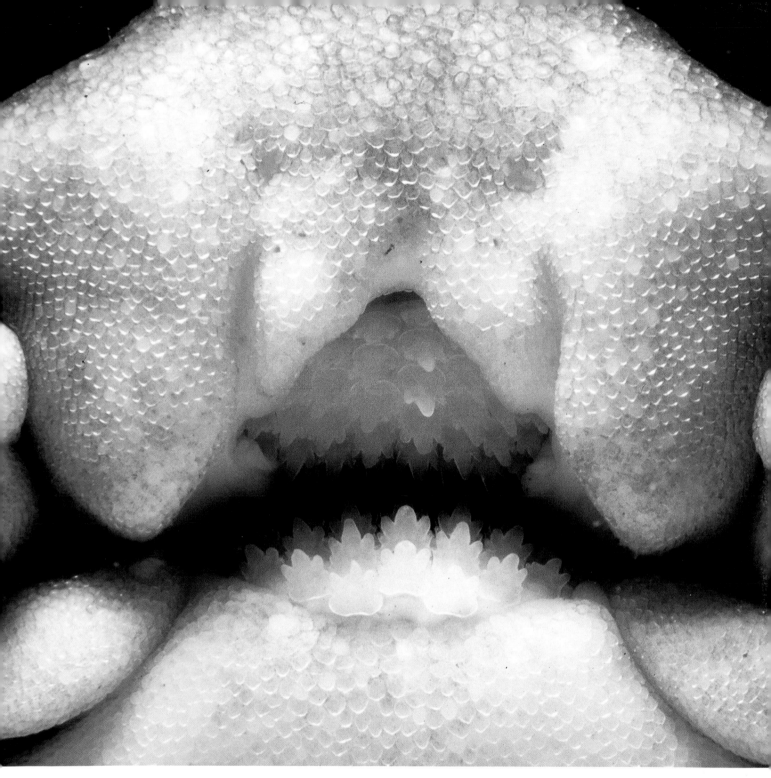

the teeth and jaws of a California hornshark

The California hornshark lives a very similar life to the Port Jackson shark. It feeds on shellfish, which it catches with small, sharp teeth at the front of its jaws, and then crushes with ridged, grinding teeth farther back. Like the epaulette shark, it is able to "walk" over the seabed, using its specially strengthened pectoral fins as legs. It lays eggs in twisted, spiral-shaped egg cases, which the female carries around in her mouth until she finds a suitable crack in a rock, where she leaves the eggs to develop.

ANGEL SHARKS AND SAW SHARKS

Angel sharks have flattened bodies and big winglike fins. They are among the smallest sharks.

Saw sharks have long sawlike snouts lined with sharp teeth.

With their flattened bodies, big, winglike fins, and eyes on the top of their heads, angel sharks look more like rays — flat-bodied relatives of sharks — than true sharks. They spend much of their lives lurking near the seabed, sometimes almost completely covered in sand or mud. They feed mostly on fish, such as plaice and sole, as well as on crabs and other shellfish, which they detect with the aid of **barbels**, fingerlike flaps around their snouts.

an angel shark, with barbels clearly visible

a well-concealed angel shark lying half-buried on the seabed, watching for prey

Saw sharks have long, sawlike snouts, lined with sharp teeth. They plough their snouts through the weeds on the seabed in search of prey, and may also attack fish by lashing at them with their "saws." A saw shark pup is born with its "saw" folded back so that it doesn't hurt its mother during birth. The snout straightens out soon afterward.

GROUND SHARKS

Ground sharks have two back fins, an anal fin, and a short mouth.

a tiger shark

There are about 200 species of ground sharks. Some of the fiercest of all sharks belong to this group. The tiger shark is a dangerous hunter which can grow to more than 20 feet long. It lives in **tropical** seas, where it hunts turtles, birds, and fish. Tiger sharks will also seize carrion. Known as the garbage cans of the sea, these scavengers have been found with some very strange objects in their stomachs, including raincoats, cans of food, lumps of coal, and tennis shoes! They get their names from the tigerlike stripes that cover their bodies when they are young. These stripes fade as the shark reaches adulthood.

a curious bull shark nudging a cage protecting divers

a lemon shark hovering above a bed of sea grass

The bull shark is a very unusual ground shark. It can survive in freshwater as well as in the sea. Because they live in lakes and rivers, bull sharks are likely to come across humans. They are extremely aggressive and there have been many reports of attacks.

A less fearsome ground shark is the lemon shark. A slow-moving, sluggish fish, it lives around mangrove swamps or beds of sea grass where it preys on fish, octopus, and crabs. Its fine, sharp teeth are ideal for grasping its slippery victims.

Requiem sharks

There are more than 50 different kinds of requiem sharks, which all belong to the ground shark group. They all have particularly sleek, streamlined bodies. The blue shark is a perfect example of this type of fish. Jacques Cousteau, a famous diver, called it "the most majestic of all sharks." The blue shark is named for the brilliant blue color of its sides and back.

One of the most common requiem sharks is the whitetip reef shark, which lives around coral reefs in the Pacific and Indian oceans. This shark spends most of the day resting in caves or rock crevices, but at night it becomes a savage hunter, ferociously tearing apart coral to reach any fish and shellfish hiding there. Another requiem shark is the silvertip, which has a stouter, heavier body than the whitetip and grows to about 10 feet long. All of its fins, except the smaller of the two back fins, are tipped with white.

a pack of whitetip reef sharks on a nighttime hunt

a silvertip accompanied by pilot fish, waiting to snap up scraps from the silvertip's meals

While sharks, such as whitetips, are resting during the day, tiny "cleaner" fish nibble small creatures, called **parasites**, from their skin. Both benefit — the cleaner fish get a meal and the big predator gets cleaned up — so the shark rarely attacks its tiny helpers.

Hammerhead sharks

Although the hammerhead shark is a ground shark, it is unique in having a head that extends to the sides, making a shape that looks like a hammer. There is one nostril and one eye on each side of the hammerhead shark's head. Some scientists think this positioning may make the hammerhead shark's senses of sight and smell more effective. Others believe that the hammer-shaped head helps the shark to steer.

There are nine different kinds of hammer-head sharks. The great hammerhead is the largest. It grows to more than 20 feet long and feeds mainly on large fish called stingrays. The scalloped hammerhead swims in **schools** of several hundred and grows to over 13 feet in length.

a group of little barber fish cleaning a scalloped hammerhead

DOGFISH, FRILLED SHARKS, AND SIX-GILLED SHARKS

Dogfish are mostly bottom-living sharks with two fins on the back and no anal fin.

Frilled and six-gilled sharks have six or seven gill slits instead of the usual five.

There are more than 100 species of dogfish. The dogfish group includes the bramble shark, lantern shark, and roughshark. Dogfish sharks generally live in deep water in temperate or polar seas. Some, like the lantern shark, attract prey in the dark depths by using light organs on their undersides. Most dogfish sharks are small, although one, the sleeper shark, can reach 20 feet in length. Many dogfish sharks have surprisingly long lives. White spotted spurdogs often live to the age of 70.

a lantern shark

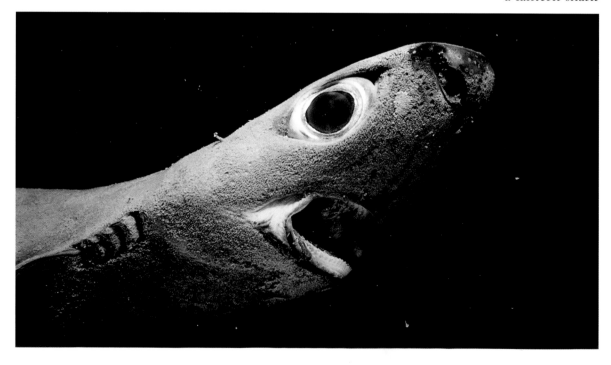

Perhaps the most unusual of all the dogfish is the cookie-cutter shark, which has a very special way of feeding. Its sharp-toothed jaws act just like a kitchen pastry cutter. It latches onto the side of much larger prey, swivels itself around, and takes a bite!

Frilled sharks, six-gilled sharks, and seven-gilled sharks generally live in deep water. As their name suggests, six-gilled sharks and seven-gilled sharks have more than the usual five gill slits. These fish are thought to be the most ancient of all sharks.

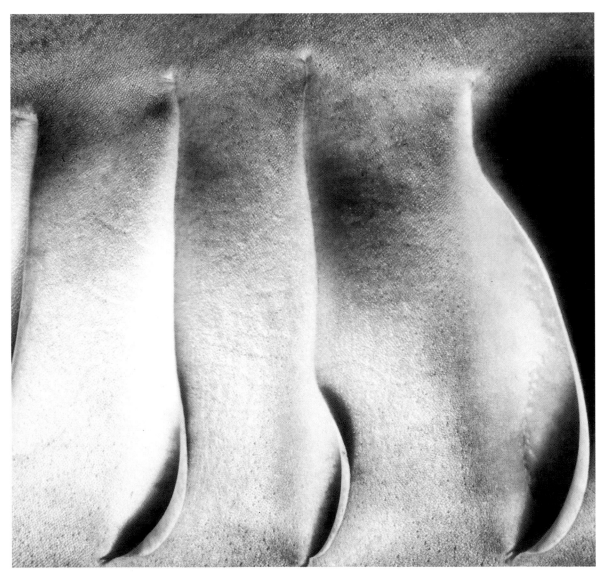

Most sharks have five gill slits, but some have four, six, or seven.

FACT FILE

• The biggest shark is the whale shark, which is at least 40 feet long when fully grown. Some specimens reach 60 feet in length and can weigh as much as 20 tons.

• A great white's tooth can measure as much as 3 inches.

• One of the smallest sharks is the spined pygmy shark. It is only 10 inches long.

• The biggest predatory shark is the great white. It can grow up to 30 feet long.

• More than half the known species of sharks are less than 3 1/2 feet long.

• During its lifetime, a shark may have as many as 20,000 teeth.

• The first sharks lived about 400 million years ago, long before the first dinosaurs.

• Eighty percent of shark species have never attacked humans.

• A great white shark eats about 11 tons of food each year.

• A shark may have up to as many as 3,000 teeth at one time.

• Sharks live in every ocean, as well as in a few rivers and lakes.

• Sharks do not have bones. Their skeletons are made of flexible, gristly cartilage.

• A shark's skin is very tough because it is covered with tiny toothlike structures.

• The fastest shark is the mako, which can swim at speeds of at least 21 miles per hour and perhaps as much as 55 miles per hour.

Ampullae of Lorenzini
Special sense organs that enable a shark to feel the tiny electrical charges given off by all living things.

anal fin
A fin on the underside of a fish near its tail.

back fin
A fin on the back of a fish (also known as the dorsal fin).

barbels
Small fingerlike flaps found on the snouts of some sharks that help the shark to sense tiny vibrations in the water and locate prey.

camouflage
The color or patterning of an animal that allows it to hide by blending with its surroundings.

carnivore
An animal that feeds on other animals.

carrion
The flesh of dead animals.

cartilage
A strong but flexible material, also known as gristle. A shark's skeleton is made of cartilage, as are people's ears and nose.

cold-blooded
Most sharks are cold-blooded, like reptiles. This doesn't mean that their blood is always cold; it means that they are only ever as warm as the temperature of their surrounding environment.

dorsal fin
A fin on the back of a fish.

gill rakers
Tiny toothlike structures inside a shark's gills, which sieve food from the water.

gill slit
The opening through which water passes from a shark's gills to the outside.

gills
Blood-filled structures with which a fish can remove oxygen from the water. The oxygen passes from the gills into the fish's blood.

krill
Tiny shrimplike creatures, which are eaten by whale, basking, and mega-mouth sharks.

lateral line system
A row of sensitive nerve endings running along each side of a shark's body. The lateral line helps the shark sense any movement in the water.

mammal
A warm-blooded animal with two or four legs and a covering of hair that gives birth to fully formed live young. Some mammals, such as whales, seals, and sea lions, have adapted to live in the sea and have flippers instead of legs.

nictitating membrane
An extra eyelid that protects a shark's eye, especially when it goes in for a kill.

parasite
An animal that spends most of its life on or inside another living creature and depends on it for food.

pectoral fins
The pair of fins on a fish's sides.

pelvic fins
The pair of fins on the underside of a fish, usually below the pectoral fins.

placenta
An organ that transfers food and oxygen from a pregnant mother to the baby inside her, and waste products from the child back to the mother.

plankton
Tiny plants and animals that float in seawater.

predator
A fish or other animal that hunts and kills other creatures to eat.

prey
Any fish or animal that is hunted and eaten by other creatures.

school
The name given to a group of fish.

species
A particular type of animal. Members of the same species can mate and produce young that are able to breed with one another.

spy hopping
When an animal raises its head out of the sea in order to locate prey, such as seals, on the shore. Great whites are the only sharks known to do this.

tail fin
The large fin at the end of a fish's tail that drives the fish forward.

temperate
Areas of the world with cool winters and warm summers. Temperate seas are cooler than tropical waters, but not as cold as polar seas.

tropical
The area around the equator where it is hot all year-round.

vertebrate
An animal with a backbone. Fish, reptiles, amphibians, birds, and mammals are all vertebrates.

Text by Jinny Johnson
The publishers wish to thank the following for the use of pictures:
BBC Natural History Unit, pp: 5 (Dan Burton); 3 (Jeff Foott); 8, 9t, 15 (Jurgen Freund); 1rhs, 24 (David Hall); 27, 36 (Brent Hedges); 11, 42 (Avi Klapfer); 26 (Conrad Maufe); back cover br (Michael Pitts); 28 (Bruce Rasner); 1, 2, 4, 6, 7, 9b, 10, 11, 12, 13b, 14b, 16, 17, 18, 19, 20, 21, 22, 23, 25, 28, 29, 30, 31, 32, 33, 34, 35, 37, 38, 39, 40, 41, 42, 43, 44, 45, front cover and back cover tl (Jeff Rotman); 14t (Geoff Simpson); 13tl (Doc White).